D1668975

Mother's Day
Notebook

Date _____

Date

Date

Date _____

Date _____

Date

Date _____

Date

Date

Date

Date

Date

Date

Date

Date _____

Date ————————————

Date _____

Date _____

Date ―――――――――――

Date _____

Date _____

Date

Date ——————————

Date

Date

Date ——————————

Date ——————————

Date

Date

Date

Date

Date

Date _____

Date

Date _____

Date _____

Date

Date _____

Date ————————————

Date ──────────────

Date ——————————

Date

Date ———————

Date ——————————————

Date

Date ——————————

Date ——————————

Date ―――――――――――

Date _____

Date _____

Date

Date

Date ——————

Date

Date

Date _____

Date _____

Date

Date ——————————

Date ——————————

Date ————————————

Date _____

Date ——————————

Date

Date

Date

Date

Date

Date ——————————

Date

Date

Date

Date

Date _____

Date _____

Date

Date

Date

Date —————————

Date _____

Date ——————————

Date _____

Date

Date _____

Date ————————

Date _____

Date _____

Date

Date _____

Date

Date _____

_____

_____

Date

Date

Date

Date

Date _____

Date

Date ——————————

Printed in Poland
by Amazon Fulfillment
Poland Sp. z o.o., Wrocław

34474066R00057